Bees In My Bonnet

A collection of Poetry

by

Isabella Strachan

ChapBook series published by:

Pipers' Ash

www.supamasu.com

CHIPPENHAM ◆ WILTSHIRE ◆ ENGLAND
SN15 4BW

Salisbury Edition
ISBN 1-902628-37-3

Bees In My Bonnet

Contents

Emotions

Parting

If you would go unbruised into the night,
Remaining neither ignorant nor bland,
As passion's out of fashion, do not say,
'This hour is God sent,' but instead
Tell over times you've been misled.
Read up research to understand
Attraction's nature; rise above
Those feelings that relate to love.

Best to have somebody with whom you share
Nothing at all; who has not read a line
That you can quote, who met and talked with you
Somewhere you'll never see again.
Whose smiling face means less to you
Than any passing stranger's may.
For whom, in short, you do not care,
And would at any time resign.

And then you'll find you part as easily
As rain from cloud or dream from sleeping brain.
For otherwise, like Furies, memory
Will track you down until you let
Go everything except you met
In such a place, looked, spoke, held hand.
Awhile like wine you drank delight,
But now it's swallowed up in sand.

Aran Islander

A young wife peels potatoes
on an island full of stones.
Fields splashed with cranesbill
red as altar wine.

She listens to the sea wind,
muffled by the reeds
between the house and sky.
The bed has new white sheets.

The Irish in her mind
is like a wedding song.

The peel smells of seaweed,
sand settles in the bowl.
Nearby, a porcelain figure;
Our Lady of the Wrecks.

Across the bay is Galway.
Ahead, America.

Her man draws in his fishing nets
beyond the island's shadow.

Persephone

She had no intimation of the search.
The advertising and broadcast appeals;
her face shown somewhat younger than it was
(her mother always saw her as a child)
Unschooled, she learned dark lessons fast.
'I'm your uncle,' he said, 'and this is our secret.'

She had little hunger all this time,
despite the foods of strange texture and taste
dug out of the earth. Onions, braised and sweet,
with long smooth leeks, obscenely shaped.
Brown nuts in casings that resembled grubs -
the nuts themselves when stripped were white and good.
Things greenless, sinister, dislodged by pigs.
They came to her upon a silver dish.
For he was rich, he said, more wealthy than a king.
She wore a fine-wrought collar, bangles and rings
and wished for strawberries in an earthen bowl.

Today, in a shallow golden cup
he sent a fruit uncoloured by the sun.
With it a sharp knife suited to her hand.
She breathed the summer apple scent
which brought back orchard, garden plot and hearth,
and stubble fields and winnowing of grain.
The baking days, the poppy-seeded loaves.
Her mother muffled with a veil
against the soft swarm of the bees;
hexagonals of the brimming comb.

The fig her mother pollinated,
subjected to the wild male tree.
The union's bloomed fruit, set beside
a bunch of corncockle and pheasant's eye.

Her mother had warned of poison fruits.
But she was grown-up now and took the risk.
She broke off seven glassy seeds
and put them in her mouth.

Infatuation

The waste of loving in an empty time
Left me hungover after I awoke.
It was no better than a pantomime,
Revolving round the central, cruel joke.
Youthful imagination made of one
Who lacked all understanding, honour, sense,
Faith, kindness, honesty, a paragon,
His qualities disguised by reticence.
And so the thought of him was long excused;
'He truly loved me, grieved to let me go -'
Until at last I saw how I'd been used,
And wondered how I ever stooped so low
As even to caress his shameless head.
Thank Heaven, though, I kept him from my bed.

Dedications

The first one says:
'From your loving husband.'
The second:
'With love and best wishes from your husband.'
I asked him for both books.
They were bought three years apart.
I compare the dedications.
I have no more of his writing.
There was no need of love-notes - all was settled
within a month of our meeting.

'Your loving husband' - that's warm and happy.
Written the year of our marriage.
'Love and best wishes' - that's more formal.

There was no cooling off.
I remember the last days.
And, sooner than believe otherwise, I'd throw out the
books,
though both are lovely and one is poetry.

I replace them gently on their shelves.

Lovers

Watching his legions at the boundary
north of the Stanegate and Pons Aelius,
the turfed wall, monument to Hadrian,
his thoughts like swallows flew to Italy,
where sunset fades to fireflies' drifting veil;
and to the youth, the Grecian nonpareil,
who'd be his naked soul's companion
for ever when time turned Elysian.
Till then he dreamed of Aphrodite's son,
who ruled his Roman heart as Antinous.

Welshman on a Train

The Greek male beauty, cut in stone,
defies the natural law.
His youth and vigour stay intact
while flesh returns to dust.

The man beside the window spoke,
his hazel eyes alight.
The ice of years cracked and broke
beneath the human sun.

I gazed upon the living face,
a man, not an ideal.
Some two millennia younger than
the marble masterpiece.

I'd like to have a Celtic head
in bronze with silver hair.
One that I could hold and stroke,
unlike the antique bust.

Shipboard Romance

She sat and watched the coast draw near,
turning the betrothal ring that bound her to
an older man, both wealthy and secure.
'Power's the best love potion,' her mother said,
busy with her embroidery.
This marriage was her parents' wish.
'She is heart whole,' they said, and so she was,
until embarking on this ship.

She'd sat up late last night while songs were sung,
moving knights and pawns upon a board.
Watching her companion's play, she thought
of the rough young men she knew at home,
their loudness, quarrelling and boasts.
What fate had brought him here to share
this little space where all could learn
each other's minds before they came to land,
a broken necklace, never to be rejoined?

The hour was quiet, as in the time
when sainted men in coracles crossed the seas
from Brittany to Cornwall, and there built
thatched oratories in soft bright grass
with flowers like candle flames. Soon she would stand
before an altar and a priest, and swear
the love and faithfulness that had changed,
like gulls from winter into spring.

She saw him now approaching, with a cup
shaped like the chalice of the Holy Grail.
'I have some wine,' he said, 'brought from Bordeaux.
Wine makes the heart rejoice, so let us drink
to married happiness.' His face was pale.

'Wine?' Iseult said. That would be unwise.
Making her stumble, reel or even laugh
wildly and without restraint so Mark's men stared
and muttered that this dark-haired Irish girl
would bring dishonour to the Cornish court.
So be it, let it rest with God!

She took the silver cup, then passed it back to him.
Each saw the other's face as though a glass
had shown it rather than their own.
Clouds streamed like floating foam: the sails
drew with the morning wind. Far away was heard
the first bars of the Liebestod.

The Love Spot
from the Irish

Three hunters in old Ireland
came to a wizard's hall.
They dined and then retired to bed
with all their host could give.
Each man was handsome, strong and tall,
but more than thirty-five.

A young girl came to share their room.
She seemed a candle's gleam.
Her beauty shone upon the wall
and kept the men awake.
She lay down in an empty bed
like full moon on a lake.

The oldest man went to her side,
and asked her for her love.
She touched the grey hairs on his head
and answered with disdain.
'I once belonged to you,' she said,
'and never will again.'

A man a little younger came
and, leaning, kissed her cheek.
She touched the grey hairs on his head
and answered with disdain.
'I once belonged to you,' she said,
'and never will again.'

Dermot O'Dyna then arose,
and offered her his love.
He went with shyness to her bed,
the nonsuch of Erin.
She touched his dark and curling hair
and stroked his glowing skin.

'I once belonged to you, Dermot,
and never can again.
For I am Youth, I tell you truth,
and I will give you this.'
A love spot came upon his brow;
she sealed it with a kiss.

So women fell in love with him,
as long as he did live.
And let his story pass the time
for men of thirty-five.

For Sheila

She went to live in Hereford
that stands beside the Wye.
I made the long train journey
Because of friendship's tie.

We walked among the Marcher hills
and saw Tintern Abbey.
I never laughed again so much
as at her comedy.

Before long she found a husband,
afterwards so did I.
We shared a rare good fortune
in our felicity.

Our letters grew less frequent,
the years began to fly.
Thomas Hardy, DH Lawrence
recall her memory.

When news came of her illness
there seemed no need to cry.
The Health Service does wonders;
surely she wouldn't die.

I've visited the cathedral
that looks across the Wye.
But not the Quaker burial ground
wherein her ashes lie.

The Ballad of Arlette

She plunged her arms into the running brook.
They and her upper bosom in the light
Of June sunshine were golden-flecked like cream.
Her curly hair shone chestnut bright.
Duke Robert fixed her with his look.

The linen lifted from the wilful water
Was spread on streamside flowers till it dried.
He spoke to one near him who'd know her name.
'What maid is that?' The man replied,
'Arlette, the tanner's daughter.'

She knew that if she fled across the ford
He might hold back, might even let her go.
But if they met it would be wolf and lamb.
Anger is sin, and sin means punishment. So,
Gently, for his soul, she greeted her lord.

Out of that gentleness there came
The Conqueror's troops on Sussex battlefield,
Homesteads and granaries given to the flame,
Saxon outlaws who died rather than yield -
She should have hanged herself for shame.

Scandal

I hadn't been born when Helen of Troy eloped,
nor when Medea bewitched Jason;
nor when all Jerusalem heard
that David had taken Bathsheba;
nor when, in Alexandria,
Cleopatra seduced Mark Antony.

Nor did I live in Rome
during the Borgia Papacy;
nor heard the first rumour
that King Henry would marry again;
nor turn out for the latest lady
approved by Charles the Second.

I don't even remember
Edward and Mrs Simpson.

But there'll always be some scandal,
like a lushly smelling flower;
and its petals from long ago
still retain the scent.
Bringing the joy and relish
of other people's sex.

Invaders

When the glazed cup was brought to shore,
blue as the dolphined sea,
it came with tales of those who lived
beside the Nile with jackal gods.
Whose inner organs after death
were sealed away in jars.

Those were times when goodwill flew
with northward cranes, and welcome broke
like flowers through turf; and sooner would
the Cretan men believe their king
held in a maze a bellowing Thing
of monstrous birth, half man, half bull,
than that one day the earth be full
and people go from land to land,
across the seas, even through the sky,
to shout and gape and laugh and chew
and trample shrines like unfrocked priests
before at last they all moved on
to violate another's ground.

Nor that the owners of the land
would bow and scrape and speak soft words
while offering cloths and ornaments,
cheap pots and knives, sunhats and charms
and dubious messages on sherds.

Canute

Retired from sea, I walked along the shore
(the land-bound flatterers following) and saw
above the high tide line that flowers grew
white as the foam or amber, purple, blue.
One striped like flags, another purest gold.
Some holding spiny spears, bristling and bold.
And leaves and stalks whose crisp and toothsome green
is with broiled herring, crab and flounders seen.
But where the busy shingle starts to ply
was spread a mass of fronds that never dry.
The flowers were gems, the others combed out wool,
folded and laid by rock and ledge and pool.
Now, as I studied nature's handiwork,
a courtier's voice aroused me with a jerk.
'The sea advances; do not fear,' he cried.
'Our wise Canute can even turn the tide!'
I stopped to let the water try to reach
my cloak's border as I stood on the beach.
At first it seemed worthwhile, seeing each clown
in fear lest he would have to watch me drown.
The moving waters knew their limits set.
The wracks would float, the flowers escape the wet.
But I was soaked and cold, left wondering
if blame be due to courtiers or to king.

Mao and the Sparrows
A tale of modern China

While the factories throb and hum
And workers in their flat caps come
Along the streets on bicycles;
To those who through the subtext steer,
Within the channel of the ear
Grace notes fall in trickles.

The garden warblers sang at dawn,
And novice monks suppressed a yawn
While chanting to the Buddha.
Stridulant, with crooked knee,
Countrywide, in field and tree,
Grasshopper and cicada.

The bronze bells with their double chime
That rang throughout the Grand Khan's time,
And jade's evergreen tone: what a
Usurping clash of pan on pan!
Enough to shake a Tang or Han
Army of terracotta.

Painters of birds in blue and rose
Despised those clouds of brown sparrows
In whose fright the noon grew dim.
From roof and barn by clangour driven,
To order of the Son of Heaven,
Close buttoned up in denim.

The inferno done, the instruments
Of state put down their implements
After the despot's rages.
But as the day's new silk unreeled,
Each cultivated flower revealed
The wisdom of the sages.

In the goldfish tank of night
Moon and stars slant on the sight
Of tiger, deer and panda.
Tired office staff and lovers meet
Beneath the dragon's glare, to eat
In palace and pagoda.

Haggard's Africa

Brought into our living-rooms:
flood, drought and famine, tyrant's rule,
land-mines and mutilated children,
wars, Aids and persecution,
poaching of rare animals.
Only, as people vote or reap their harvests,
Africa rejoices.

But, in books,
school prizes, bought secondhand,
with embossed covers, illustrations
and names of extinct publishers;
on library shelves, reissued paperbacks with lurid covers,
there is another Africa.

Without workers or peacekeepers,
or friends of silverback gorillas,
or even civilising missions.
Men with Victorian self-centredness
carrying Winchester rifles, bent on quests
for treasure or lost peoples or big game,
or vanished wives or brothers.

Hunter Quatermain comes first,
in search of Solomon's mines.
The mountain crossing, the moon's eclipse,
the petrified kings' corpses.
Imprisonment in the diamond cave.
And, after many another yarn
of holy flower, ivory child,
his wives, Marie and Stella,
Zu-Vendis and the love-struck queens.

Then the other races.
The warrior, Umslopogaas,
and Nada, lily of death.
The Zulu armies and their kings.
Heroism of Voortrekker and Boer.
Tales of colonial times, history passed over
by Mandela's rainbow nation.
Rider Haggard made of it
a darkness like a tropic sky
lit by meteors.

Most of all, the work that haunts
and brings one back to read again
the Sherd of Amenartas.
Through storms and swamps to ruined Kôr,
with caves of fair mummies.
She who had lived two thousand years
behind a veil, for love's return.
Her beauty in the living fire
that shrivelled her with age...

Africa took him.
Writer and public servant.
Home again in Norfolk
he gave his Africa to us.

Field Poppy

Flowers of war dead:
scarlet poppies in the field,
wreathing cenotaphs.

Nimrud and Nineveh at the British Museum

Assyria was a war machine;
its name hissed by its chariot wheels,
the Nazis of antiquity.
Huge bovine guards of glossy black,
reliefs of warriors, heads in heaps;
monuments to monstrous kings.
Engraved panels from Nineveh
and Nimrud line the walls
of basement and ground floor.

We've been through the killing fields,
likewise the Holocaust.
We've seen too much of genocide
for half a century.
It might be better to find some crates,
sort out the best, put in the rest;
return them to Iraq.

Wartime Mother

We fetched up in a northern town,
like driftwood among the ironware on the shore
we gathered when the cruel sea retreated,
to supplement the dusty, slate-mixed coal.
Such fires burnt out before the time for bed.

The wartime summers were hot - we sunbathed in the dunes.
My youngest loved the sea's edge and living sands.
The elder rode her bicycle before the wind
along the promenade.

'Children in Europe would be glad of this,' I said,
as again they turned from the reconstituted meal
that tasted like pulped paper.
We forced down meat of doubtful provenance,
laughed at the cookery hints - 'Add codliver oil to the mash' -
the laughter grew hysterical. Boredom was more frequent.
Books with blurred print, few toys in the shops,
the damp hours below ground when the siren howled;
the girls wanted the war to end
no less than the rest of us.

At night, drawing a curtain across the blind
to shut out a night too full of stars
(down the coast a solitary light
brought death and smoking ruins before the dawn),
in dreams I fed them buttered toast and new-laid eggs,
lamb from New Zealand, fruit from Africa,
filled them with sugar or chocolate.
Goods brought on voyages through peaceful seas,
over sunken ships, unconsecrated tombs.

Timor Mortis

You who are the living
have taken our possessions.
Taken what was left with us
for our consolation.

We who reached adulthood,
felt and thought like you,
are stripped and left to wander
within these lumber rooms.

We are the ancient dead.
Our gods are overthrown.
Our priests and seers discredited.
Our seed scattered and lost.

Those still remained to us,
the gifts of sons and daughters,
of lovers and of friends.
The work of our best craftsmen
was put within our reach.

We cannot eat together
or drink our wine or ale
from beakers of black and chestnut
or white Cycladic stone,
cups flowered with pictures
that show the world we knew;
glassware green as seawater,
leaf brown or springflower blue -
for Nubians, Greeks, Italians,
or warriors from the Rhine.

Vessels that were chosen,
placed, flawless and unbroken,
tenderly with the dead.

See our inwrought ornaments,
badges of wealth and rank.
Beads brought by the merchantmen,
gold discs and filigree,
berries, beetles, bees,
reminders of the sun.

Offerings for our women.
Spindles and their whorls,
combs and jewellery boxes,
rainbow perfume bottles,
palettes to mix cosmetics,
for beauty's summertime.

Evenings here are quiet.
Those we left remembered
throwing dice with us.
Boards and gaming pieces
would pass away the time.

The museum doors swing open,
high windows blue the day.
Faces alive and eager
throng round our images
in wood, marble, basalt.
The dried-up, crouching figure
from predynastic sands.

The sacrificial victim
hauled out of a bog.
And hacked-off, plastered skulls
with cowrie shells for eyes.

Now in our desolation
we seek to take revenge.
Most people pass too quickly
to know that we are here.

But sometimes there's a visitor
whom we have seen before.
Who lives in the philosophy
which comes when youth is gone.

We'd like to approach and whisper
the wisdom of our age:
'Tokens of grace and splendour
in substance and in shape,
were given for distraction
against the fear of death.'

We watch your breathing flood
in flush of warmth and health.
Look at your dress and footwear,
the toys that mark your hours.
And say, though no one hears us,
'You too will come to dust.'

Christianity

Mary

She swapped the simple life
of a Nazareth housewife
for talk with an angel
confinement in a stable
water turned to wine
a sword through the soul
and a galaxy of images
human and divine.

The Governor's Wife

Now at last the afternoon is silent;
The sentence given, the man taken away,
The people gone to celebrate their feast
Of Passover; it marks a time, they say,
When with their faceless God, long years ago,
They brought down plagues upon the land of Pharaoh.
This place is full of tales. Now I can rest,
Although I think the man was innocent.

My husband said he had to give assent
To the man's death, and that his hands are clean
Of blood; that he attempted a release,
And it was his affair. What did I mean?
To execute a man is men's business,
And a woman's to ask for gentleness,
For nothing more than her own inward peace.
Yet I do think the man was innocent.

I lately heard the sound of merriment
Following a donkey through the city.
That was an entry for a king! To go
With trodden branches and hosanna cry.
But why should Romans care? A carpenter
A threat to Caesar? Tell me another!
Even a woman can see through that. So
I still believe the man was innocent.

He's drinking wine with friends now, well content
At trouble over, able to take breath.
My head is aching and I hope this night
May pass more easily. A nasty death -
But not women's business, except for those
Who see it carried out. How dark it grows!
So much the better, blotting out the sight
Of that good man I know was innocent.

Summary Execution

The prisoner saw the moonlight fall
on water in a bowl; he dipped his hand
as he had done in Jordan's shallow stream.
Drops beaded heads and backs while voices spoke
of minor sins, temptations of slight lives.
Before those days he lived with innocents.
The desert beasts, gazelle and horned oryx,
foxes and conies of the rocks, the badger,
his rival for the wild bees' nest.
And once the scapegoat, banished from its flock
fierce-eyed and frightened, fled at his approach.
He watched the kite and vulture at their work,
seeing how they cleansed the desert land.
Far off, a city's towers and palaces,
where people gamed and drank, like those
whose shouts and laughter came tonight,
faint down the prison shaft.

Isaiah's heir, crying in the wilderness.
The other, his kinsman, among his friends
had come for baptism with the crowds.
He dealt with country folk and learned Jews,
not jumped-up Edomites, the chief of whom
now held his birthday feast above.
God knew the fates awaiting them
and how they'd fit their different lives.
The one who shunned the cities and their kings,
whose ways were outside politics, and the one
who spoke against corruption in high places.

The round moon filled the bowl; the guests
were quiet. A catlike girl, half naked, stared,
astonished at the careless oath.
Her mother waited for the silenced head.
The silver dish was large enough
to keep the blood from dripping on the floor.
Herod hid his face, an axe changed hands.
And indrawn breath sounded throughout the room
like desert wind across the midnight sands.

New Worship

Now, for the benefit of empty pews,
A flower arrangement glows upon a stand.
Untimely death pervades the daily news,
With shop-wrapped flowers and messages by hand.
For sorrow pictured on the tabloid page
For innocence destroyed or beauty dead,
New times decree a new style pilgrimage,
Not hymn nor psalm with consecrated bread.
No risen Saviour can bring relief.
For loss of one, young, shining, undefiled,
A teddy bear is icon of belief,
While virgin mother mocks the murdered child.
The Gospel teaching is perused in vain
When public grief dissolves in private pain.

Santa Claus
Metropolitan Cathedral, Liverpool

Below the tower of many-coloured glass
on fabric hanging is Saint Nicholas.
He's Santa Claus to families of the north.

To earn his name for generosity,
he surely spent his fourth-century day
not merely countering heresy.
His church being rooted, he could put forth
the fair white flowers of charity.
His resurrection of three little boys,
the maids who wed with his dowry,
the sailors saved from death at sea;
are those who blessed good Bishop Nicholas.

Translated now to ride a jingling sleigh,
white-bearded with sack of tinselled toys,
through him our trusting children see
their elders' shameless perfidy.

Dissenting Faith

I think of churches, plain and stern
I've seen in Scotland, Holland, Germany.
Of Bunyan's pilgrims, and America
in times of Hawthorne, Alcott, Emerson.
Of Milton's vision of the Fall of Man,
and hymns of Wesley, Luther, Whittier.
Dissenting faith like a refiner's fire,
beyond processions, images and saints.

If this had been my childhood gift,
I might have seen it bright and clear,
a vessel strong and hard as glass,
and learned to love austerity.
Instead, my faith's a leaky bowl,
with buried bulbs that will not show
their shafts of living green, nor lift
a honey-scented corymb to the light.

Caedmon (AD 680)

Caedmon the herdsman,
Keeper of cattle,
Worker at Whitby,
Fled from the feasting.
Hid in the stable,
Hating the harp song.
Fearing the mockery
Over the mead horn
Of the Northumbrians.

There in the beasts' byre,
Asleep in the straw,
His name called at midnight,
'Sing me a song.'
'I'm not a singer,'
Caedmon said crossly.
'That's why I left the hall
Before the harp reached me.'

'But you shall sing to me,'
So said the stranger
Standing in a stall.
'Sing of the Creation'

Under the night sky
Wrought as a rooftree,
Caedmon sang of the Lord;
Of the world's warden,
Wonderful in wisdom,
His glory supernal.
And when he was woken
By the lamp lit in heaven,
His soul kept the anthem
As the monks' lettering,
Jewel-like and glittering.

Art and Imagination

The Winged Victory of Samothrace

I stand upon a public stair;
The people crowd to see me there.
My sculptor gave me cygnet's wings
And blew my robe back from my knee;
My torso as a wild bird sings.
They call me the Winged Victory.

Once a girl, a swallow in flight,
I raced my friends in morning light.
The sculptor saw me breast the wind.
He caught my spirit as I passed;
With his Greek genus aligned
He shut it in a marble cast.

A sign to sailors, scudding by,
Constant beneath my island sky,
Until I fell, lying broken,
Still in my marmoreal grace.
Then to the shore came thieving men,
Who took me from the sea-god's place.

A damaged thing beyond repair:
The people come in flocks to stare.
Unsatisfied, they go their way,
For none has ever seen my face.
Yet beauty's rapine I repay;
In Paris as in Samothrace.

Roman Mosaic

The designer speaks:

Forget the northern ocean's tide,
The coasts where sea and rocks collide.
I'll make this floor the Mediterranean,
Playground of Greek and Carthaginian;
An island's windless bay or deep inlet.
Within the mosaic I will set,
Wreathed with chalk shells a triton's head;
Fish shoals with eyes of sandstone red,
Shale and slate marking the bars
Along a mackerel back; an Attic vase
Spilled from a wreck is brushed by passing fin.
Outlined emerging, a dolphin
Carries a naked boy as rider.
Through a mirage of sunlit water
Figures are sheened as if the stones were wet.

Reclining at your exiled banquet,
Marooned in this lapidary sea,
You'll feel yourselves in Naples or Capri,
Their caverns blue in liquid light.
Thinking you've not grown old with failing sight,
Though Saxon ships along the British shore
Unload their men as you stare at the floor.

Virgil translated

A box of secondhand books
outside a charity shop.
A notice pegged to its side:
THRILLERS SCI FI CRIME
ROMANCE ACTION HUMOUR.
Among them, Virgil's *Aeneid,*
translated for easy reading.

On the busy pavement
I recalled the antique cadence -
'Infandum, regina, ubes renovare dolorem.'

Thriller? Yes, when first told
to the mixed race on the Alban Hills;
descended not only from Sabines and Latins
and almond-eyed, decadent Etruscans,
but also from Homer's Trojans.

Sci Fi? If that includes gods and goddesses,
harpies, the sea monster Scylla,
the Underworld and its ghosts.

Crime? Deceit, betrayal, selfishness -
the smoke of Dido's pyre.

Romance? The stop at Carthage ordained by the gods.
The flirtation that got out of hand.

Action? Plenty of that.
Wars and battles, voyaging, storms, escapes.

Humour? That rests with Virgil himself
(back home in Mantua, after his journey with Dante).
Smiling to himself at the sight
of his magnum opus in a later tongue,
priced in denarii.

Creation

When I saw the astronomy programme,
with its computer simulations
of the birth pangs of the cosmos,
light and heat exploding,
time and space begotten;
talk of a billion galaxies,
each with a billion stars,
sometimes the possibility
of planets with nothing but microbes,
or frozen or molten rock,
aeons and aeons away -
I shrugged as I turned off the set.
Grown tired of all the turmoil,
the explosions and glare of space-time.
The galaxies, nebulae, black holes -
in fact of the whole bang shoot.

When I stood by the glass case and saw
the lily-stemmed Greek vase,
its balletic pose, its readiness
for the jewelled splash of wine -
there in its grace and its silence,
that cup seemed the bud of the blossoming,
the point where creation began.

Historic House

The sun makes coral of the brick.
I show my card and go inside
as if this pile of history
were from a fairytale.

Follow the arrowed direction,
the thread that runs throughout the maze,
bypassing forbidden thresholds.
A brochure is the helpful guide.
The prohibition, Do Not Touch.

The saloon or living-room,
garish with gilding - panels and *torchères*
(supporting figures); a clock in ormolu,
and cabinet with satinwood inlay;
a Sèvres vase, a Chelsea figurine.
Much spoil from some Grand Tour.
There's beauty, taste and glamour,
as in a painted tomb.

Two dozen guests could use the dining-room,
with candelabra among the Meissen pieces.
For hearty drinkers, cooler, tankard, flagon.
An inspection of the kitchen, where the cook
used range and spit, copper and pewter moulds.
A mug made for the Diamond Jubilee.
This is the house's stomach, where's its heart?

In the library I take a look
at bookcases by Chippendale.
The volumes, morocco-bound, are Gibbon,
Scott, Dickens, Macaulay, Froude -
travel books, *Arabian Nights* by Burton.

Then I ascend the broad oakwood staircase.
How many feet have gone that way,
soft in kid, brocade and cloth?
(Stiletto heels are banned.)
I admire along the gallery
Louis Quinze tapestries,
a marble peruked worthy and a nude.
More from the house's store of art,
Constable, Canaletto, Coninxloo.

The bedrooms in chinoiserie
knew bought brides and sottish heirs;
death, less often from age than diseases,
obstetrics, gluttony. All's clean and bland,
kept free of dust and moth.
Cordoned off, a flight of narrow stairs
leads up to the attic,
or little rooms beneath the gables,
for fugitives to hide.

Queen Anne, the Regent, Louis Quatorze,
English, French, Italian, Dutch,
dynasties, revolutions, wars,
all laid out before our gaze.
Expensive toys on shelves and tables,
but not a child to be seen.
This is all a grown-up game,
one day lost, next day won,
in at one door, out of the same.
In an ante-room I find the prizes.
Fudge, oven gloves and Morris trays,
postcards, jams and scents in various guises.
Passions of past centuries
made pretty and domestic.

Hands

After a bath
I treat my hands
to feasts of cream
to make them soft

to make them pale
and marble smooth
then from a bowl
lift out a fruit.

Milo's Venus
has lost her hands
it's said she held
a round apple

her hands were white
and marble smooth
the loveliest hands
the world has seen.

Female Form
15th-century picture

He let me see the painting yesterday,
my part in it complete, though not the whole.
There's landscape detail still to be filled in:
a winding road, three knights riding thereon,
cypress and towered castles on a hill.
Nearer, the naked baby's smile,
angels like gulls above the fishing fleet.

Mine is a standing female form,
such as these artists use to please the eye
fatigued with holiness and peasant maids
(virgin or not) posed with a lily vase,
dandling a child, trueborn or otherwise.
A square transparent veil frames my face.
A borrowed dress of dark red silk is trimmed
with plain white fur at wrist and hidden breast.
He ordered me to keep my eyes cast down
and hold my hands clasped lightly, palm to palm.

When we last met within the sheets,
he told me that he'd heard a Florentine
has shown his girl riding upon the sea,
with ropes of golden hair and nothing more,
while youths like heathen gods blow flowers on her.
If this fashion reaches our Flemish realm,
he says he'll throw away my silk and fur,
unbind my waist and free all my long hair,
and so be Master of the Female Form!
Till then he'll be content with drapery,
and I to play my part, for I know well
when that day comes he'll paint a younger girl,
while my old husband keeps me at his side.

Two pictures
from the Wallace Collection, London

1 Spanish Lady

She has a look of court lady and nun,
in black mantilla like a convent veil
and dress of cocoa brown; a matching fan
ripples like river water in the sun.
A scintilla of red repeats her lips.
Her hands are white-gloved; from her wrist a chain
suspends a cross, her people's pride and shame;
Peruvian gold and Inquisition flame.

The artist showed her shift above her breasts,
and slipped a string of jet beads round her neck.
Pale, long-nosed face and shy, half startled eyes
are set against uninterrupted dun.
No ancient rocks, no ghostly, bald-browed smile;
Velasquez knew that had been done before.
We call her merely Lady with a Fan,
a picture leaving little to explain.

2 The Laughing Cavalier

Hals' young man's face beneath his monstrous hat
is signed to elude; the mouth is stern,
the eyes ironic - his laughter contained
in oil paint dried to flower or branch or crystallise
into cuffed lace or goffered lawn.
Impatient of riddles, we prefer
abstraction, aggravation, anarchy.
Confined to its west London home,
the portrait arrests the one who sees
beyond the bedizening to find
the golden apple with the bitter rind.

To a Film Star

Not marble, nor Sargent portrait that's hung
Framed in a gallery or private room
To be exalted, rhapsodized and sung,
Remains like you, forever in full bloom.
For you have animation, sparkling eye,
Red lips that speak, laugh, coax, enslave, beguile,
Hands to caress your co-star's manly thigh,
Thick shining hair and classical profile.
You play your part upon whichever stage
The make-up artist paints you to be seen.
Neglect, abuse, disfiguring old age,
The grave itself, bows to the silver screen.
Long past the judgement that the world applies,
Your light reflects back from your public's eyes.

Sky, Land and Seascapes

Cloud

The cloud hangs, shadowless,
white as the mountain ranges far away.
At first a giant distaff
held out to catch each floating thread.
Later, a winding sheet.

Cattle stand on river beds.
Girls draw half empty buckets from the wells.
The cloud is useless, dry as marble dust.

At sunset it's bundled silk, shot pink and gold,
strung with wild swans flying to distant lakes.

The people gaze, indifferent.

They'd rather see a black and scowling mass,
and out of it their rain god,
forking the sky to bring down reviving torrents.

Bridge

The new road bridge was opened recently.
It combs the knots out of the traffic flow.
The river bulges here; across the countryside
the banks close in, yoked by a little bridge
that was not made for wheels.

A lane runs down, past houses and a church.
After the rood screen and misericords
you search out the path among the trees
leading to the medieval bridge.
No parapet occludes the downward view.
The water's bronze, with fry like blown pellets.
Upstream are mattresses of watercress.
Women once rinsed their linen at the brim.
In season now is lady's smock instead,
yellow flag, mint, balsam and meadowsweet,
flickering like print curtains in the wind.
Grey wagtails nest close by the riverbank.
In autumn there's a drift of crimson leaves.

On the farther side, the Friesian cows
come down to drink and stare; a Dutch master
would think himself back near his Haarlem home.
Beside the field's a fence; a green lane cuts
past more farmland, all part of an estate,
abbey lands under the Norman kings.
Packhorses carried salt and grain,
tallow and wool, barrels of ale and fish,
parchment and paints for the scriptorium.
Poor folk who'd had a blessing with their bread
cursed Thomas Cromwell when he came this way.

The new bridge stretches, steel-nerved.
High-sided vehicles drive over it.
The old bridge is an irrelevance.
The river as a boundary's been rubbed out;
in drought a set of stepping stones would do,
and children don't play Pooh sticks any more.
Yet somehow you're at peace, standing there,
and no one uses it for suicide.

Byroad

A bicycle best suits this country road.
Walkers tightrope its verges warily,
feet brushed by bellflowers or moon daisies.
Drivers hold wheels like riders with tight reins.
No bus stop flies its numbered flag.

Romans laid the earliest foundation,
but Saxons built no village here,
and Normans no monastery. It might
have vanished under dead-nettles, except
for the wider road that bisected it,
leading officiously towards the coast.
Its biggest upheaval was McAdam.
It missed the stagecoach, turnpike, highwayman.
Of two world wars, it witnessed nothing more
than German prisoners felling trees.

Today, unlighted, it's a safe crossing
For badger, deer and rabbit in the dusk.
In spring the cuckoo oboes over it.
Goldfinches clink like horseshoes struck with steel.
Grasses remain uncut, flowers unpoisoned.

Time's car is parked along this road.

Chalk Hill

Today the downland's springing turf
is sunned or wet with rain.
And there grow plants that love the chalk,
rock rose, bugloss, self heal.
With rabbits' feet and singing larks,
blue butterflies and bees.

But once there stretched a trackless sea
where reptiles coiled in surf;
while through its depths, unceasingly,
dead seashells fell like snow.
Till, leaving hills like monsters' bones,
the sea gave up its bed.

A walker, lying at his ease,
hears through the tickling grass
faint sounds of water, wind and tide,
the wash of vanished seas.

Winds

Summer wind in the garden
dances with washing,
broadcasts flower scents,
puts shrubs in a shiver,
refreshes and cools.

Country wind swirls away seeds,
swings on the cornstalks,
bustles through treetops,
blows butterflies sideways,
turns leaves to silver.

Autumn wind in the city
dashes rain against panes,
tumbles horse-chestnuts,
drives smoke from the bonfires,
strips back umbrellas.

River wind sways the loosestrife,
spoils the ducklings' first swim,
sings in the reed-beds,
disturbs the day's fishing,
breaks up reflections.

Shore wind expands the yachts' sails,
sighs over the saltings,
lifts sand like rough sheets,
sweeps through the sea-asters,
sets the gulls swearing.

Seawind, once, in mid-ocean,
winged clippers like swallows
on leaving Shanghai;
rushed homeward past islands,
with sweet-smelling teas.

Wide open Spaces

Some people love wide open spaces.
They talk of exhilaration under an unmeasured sky.
Some idea that this is where God lives,
God with hair like a comet.
These wide open spaces will be prairie, pampas,
savannah, steppe;
with ranchers, gauchos, Africaners, cossacks.

I have only known the Canterbury Plains.
Where I felt unimaginably far from home.
Away from the landscapes
that showed where people had lived.

I like to walk on earth that may hide tiles or awls or
beakers,
bubble over with pennies,
be patterned with gods, dolphins and fruits.
Where stones stand old and tall
and barrows hump the turf.

In the great cleanness at the edge of the world
I longed for such earth.
I took ship home, I have no regrets.
Home to the barrows and rings,
the abbeys and drystone walls,
the buildings that shelter the work of long ago craftsmen.
I left the wide open spaces
to those enamoured of emptiness,
to angels wide-winged in the empyrean,
and the interminable flocks of sheep.

Untilled Field

A field unbroken by the plough,
ungrazed by cow or sheep.
Wild mushrooms spill like silver coins,
and hares run through the dusk.
Out in the sun a fox glows red,
his tail a brushwood brand.
Sometimes a lapwing curls its crest,
or lark lets down its song.
Cowslips in spring, brown butterflies,
a bramble dark with fruit.
Nothing's allowed to vex or harm
or push the others out.
A donkey, playing bobby, curbs
the thistles' gang warfare.
May his field and fence remain
until man's day is done.

Caithness Glass

This is the land of Caithness glass,
where winter's stay is long.
Cairn, broch and ducal monument
are thatched with frozen snow.

The workers from the old Norse towns
assemble at the fire.
By skilful twists the molten glass becomes
stones moulded by the sea,
buds, flower sheaths and rigid stems,
goblets and half-moon bowls,
a glass menagerie.

They stand in rows; the thin cold light
turns glass to gemstones, such as
felspar, zircon, amethyst,
garnet, opal, tourmaline,
sapphire, golden topaz.
Although it could be cracked
like iced pools underfoot.

Border Country

A walker today may cross the Border
by an ancient bridge that loops the Tweed;
through drystone walls or along a road
where captured reivers swung in the wind.
Two kingdoms here were juxtaposed,
and a king lay dead on Flodden hill.

Red grouse whirr past a ruined keep;
a peel tower's converted to a house.
The thistles flower impartially
where skulls looked eyeless at the sky.
Now crows perch on the farmer's fence,
or share the fields of Cheviot sheep.

The smells of fear, of horse, of carrion
are replaced by those of village stores.
With crown and mace new times begin
while Andrew's saltire tops the poles.
Some children ask for Edinburgh rock,
while others want Kendal mint cake.

Fulmar

High on a steep Atlantic cliff,
so tall the brain turns at the sight,
the fulmar broods her lonely chick,
crouched on turf and sea-pink flowers;
awaiting the day when, duty done,
she lifts and planes on moth-grey wings
past rocky turrets of the coast
to find her loves, the ships that ply
among the hyperborean isles
of Orkney, Shetland, Handa, to grim
Cape Wrath. On autumn days of opal sun
she flies in search of farthest Thule
and, rounding Norway to the Arctic seas,
skims the iron circle of the Pole.

Channel Island Shells

Seashells kept in a brown glazed bowl
like heirlooms of a bygone age.
Scallops are opened fans, topshells
have colours of dead flowers, applied
as freckles or in pen-nib stripes
as though to prove a steady hand.
Thin gleaming shells like fingernails
and sea-snails, smooth and marble white.
A wendletrap within a net
laid down across its washed out spire.
These came from chilly island coasts.
Bath warm waters of ocean reefs
fix orange, yellow, red in shells,
splashed paint that won't be scrubbed away.
They're blank disks: the others recall
a seaside childhood or a day
of honeymoon. In after years,
how beautiful they are in death.

Stars

Moonless winter night.
Stars like bees on tight shut flowers,
petals indigo.

Night Piece

Figures of glass keep out the moon.
Only through clear panes it falls
into an empty, waiting font
and reads inscriptions on the walls.

Around the tower with breathless vane
and silently suspended bell,
a bat resembles in its flight
some demon shrieking out of hell.

The summer moon, mouldered and full,
rises above the black-branched yew.
Mourners' flowers are humus dark;
an angel gleams with dew.

Congregations long since gone,
clerics, choristers and children,
seem at one with soft winged moths
in light where sight's mistaken.

Viking Ship: AD 1000

We Viking ships have epic tales to tell,
when hauled up on the strand we wait for spring,
or after some long sailing are careened,
scrubbed, dried and painted, our tall masts renewed,
our sails repaired, our missing shields replaced,
the gaping dragon prow made fiercer yet.

We tracked the whale through jewelled bergs of ice,
saw flying fish like bolts of silver spray,
and anchored on green shores, where christened men
trembled in terror at the Viking name.
Or so it was some hundred years ago.
Now many of our Danish warriors
in quiet living forget their gods
to worship the White Christ upon his cross.
Berserkers browse like cattle on the fields
Alfred of Wessex gave them in years past.
While southward of the narrow water
there's easy living in the Frankish land.

Each year more pines are left to catch the snow
than cut and planed to plough the bitter seas.
Our captains fret out of unwillingness
to change their axes for a thrall's scythe,
and afterwards to lie in hogback graves.
They long for mighty plundering days; the cry,
'Lord, save us from the Northmen's fury!'
For the Valkyrie to choose them from the slain
to feast with Odin in Valhalla's halls.

But now a rumour has been spread abroad
that my captain, Leif Ericsson, will sail
towards the west, across the great ocean.
Perilous the voyage and its goal
unknown. Perhaps there's but a little isle,
like Lindisfarne of the monks' picturebook
that shows men with the sun behind their heads,
winged beasts, and writing in the Latin tongue.

Hopefully we may find a land
which seems the gods' country; where all our folk
may dine on huge salmon, roast deer and pork,
sing to the harp and quaff long drinking horns.
And at the last be buried in their ships.
Gold and silver, garnet and glass,
torque and brooch and amulet
hidden beneath the long grass of the dunes.
And if that's not to be, why then, by Thor,
We'll journey onwards till we reach the stars.

The Silk-bearers

Norman and Cynthia, our Bactrian camels,
have gone to the big field for summer

Notice at Marwell Zoo.

I followed the fence to find them.
To salute the beasts from Bactria,
which is Afghanistan.

These carried the packs of the Silk Road.
Bales of silk like morning mist
rolled from China to the West.
Being less than dainty
about their choice of greenery
and clad in hairy winter coats,
camels travelled the Central Asian highways.
Kublai Khan would have known them.

Because of their two-humped endurance,
Persia and Byzantium rode on waves of silk.
Through them China's genius came
to temper the gross appetites of the West.

I found the pair in their field.
Lolling in the fat summer grass,
like retired pillars of the community.
I hope you are happy here,
Norm and Cyn.

All Our Poets of the Seasons - 2nd Edition

THE POETRY COLLECTIONS published earlier in chapbook format are now available in one comprehensive volume containing over 800 poems showing a variety of poetical styles - an invaluable work for all new and not so new poetry lovers. The work includes:

'The Sea and Galilee' by Brian Federico. The sea and the tropical sun, and the hot nights in New Orleans, all brought to life by a young naturally born poet.

'A Web of Cries' by Dr. Pamela Bakker. After a brilliant start to her career with the BBC, Pamela was diagnosed with the severest form of M.E/C.F.S , but through her illness she experienced an outpouring of real poetry, as this moving collection shows.

'Recitable Rhymes' by Alan Millard. This is a brilliant collection of humorous poems by a witty writer which can be recited for any of many occasions.

'Travels in the Antipodes' by J. C. Ottaway. A collection of poems which takes the reader on a beautiful journey through Heaven on Earth . . .

'Desert Anthems' Poetry is the Council of the Arabs, so these works of the Immortal Arab Poets were translated by Talaal M. Omer to transport new readers into their hot, colourful, enchanting worlds.

'Augmented Seventh' by Gwyneth Hughes. Gwyneth Hughes works in the theatre in Paris, and colourfully describes her experiences through this collection of poetry.

'Southern Skies' edited by Yvonne Eve Walus. An anthology of New Zealand poets.

'Signals in the Dark' by Sylvia Downes. Revelations to stimulate the intellect as well as the emotions from a well-travelled, observant lady.

'Catch Me If You Can' by Sue Fincham. The revealing loves, the hopes, the hates, the fears, the thoughts and the yearnings of a lady who lives by the sea in beautiful Norfolk

Blinkers Off' by Jean Frances. Jean Frances was born in England and emigrated to Australia so saw her new world with new eyes. This is her heartfelt story.

'Hope to Defeat' by Rhona Johnston. Rhona Johnston was a long-distance runner who was suddenly struck down by the dreaded anorexia nervosa. In this collection of moving poems she writes despairingly and hauntingly of her spirited recovery.

The Hour-Glass' by Sarah Collett.. Sarah Collett wrote this amazing collection as a schoolgirl on the borders of Wiltshire and Gloucestershire. For one so young, she writes with intense feeling and emotion, creating words of immense power to describe the merest whispers.

'A Pillow Book' by Yvonne Eve Walus. A worthy collection of poems by the talented South African writer who remarkably, without bias or favour, has previously been published as *'Author of Our Times'* and *'Writer of the Future'*.

'Stanza Chance' by Bob Griffiths. Our first *'Poet of the Season'* in this programme is an ex-helicopter pilot from Devon whose collection shows a remarkable insight into life, love and thoughts. (The poet was invited to read his poems on Devon Radio).

'What Women Talk About' by Tonie Watts. Not only what women talk about, but what women think and what women feel, written by a woman whose intellect should not be underestimated.

'Bees in My Bonnet' by Isabella Strachan. Isabella Strachan has an uncanny aptitude for seeing everyday events in their historical perspective which adds a certain realism to this collection of poems.

'Les Deux Poetes Français'. Poet of the Season' is not one, but two poets, neither English, but both French and long since dead. But the work of the sixteenth century poets, Joachim du Bellay and Pierre Ronsard, now sensitively translated by Reine Errington, takes us into a very different country in a very different age. Yet there is something strangely familiar within their rural settings. It is like discovering an early Shakespearean manuscript.